David befriended me when I had few friends.

He led me to Christ.

He taught me how to grow in my relationship with the Lord.

We were college roommates.

We did a lot of crazy stuff together.

Do you think we were close friends? You bet we were!

Do you think we got along well with each other? No way! Sometimes we fought like two cats who had their tails tied together.

Yet today he and I remain the best of friends...

Other Here's Life books—

Friendships:

Making The Best Of Them

Bill Jones

Here's Life Publishers

First printing, August 1989
Second printing, January 1990

Published by
HERE'S LIFE PUBLISHERS, INC.
P. O. Box 1576
San Bernardino, CA 92402

ISBN 0-89840-257-3
LOC Catalog Card Number 89-83736

Scripture quotations are from *The New American Standard Bible,* © The Lockman Foundation 1960, 1962, 1963, 1968, 1971, 1972, 1975, 1977.

For More Information, Write:

Student Mission Impact – P.O. Box 2200, Stone Mountain, GA 30086
L.I.F.E. – P.O. Box A399, Sydney South 2000, Australia
Campus Crusade for Christ of Canada – Box 300, Vancouver, B.C., V6C 2X3, Canada
Campus Crusade for Christ – Pearl Assurance House, 4 Temple Row, Birmingham, B2 5HG, England
Lay Institute for Evangelism – P.O. Box 8786, Auckland 3, New Zealand
Campus Crusade for Christ – P.O. Box 240, Raffles City Post Office, Singapore 9117
Great Commission Movement of Nigeria – P.O. Box 500, Jos, Plateau State Nigeria, West Africa
Campus Crusade for Christ International – Arrowhead Springs, San Bernardino, CA 92414, U.S.A.

Contents

> *A friend loves at all times.*
> *Proverbs 17:17*

Dedicated to David Z. Cowan

You befriended me when I didn't know Jesus Christ personally and led me to Him by your life and words. You set a godly example for me to follow and have loved me unconditionally for all these years.

Thank you for being my friend.

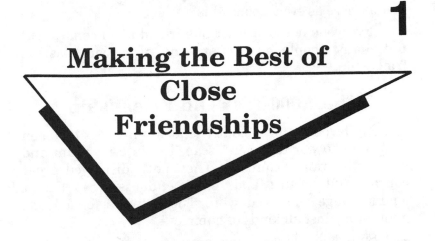

Making the Best of Close Friendships

Only his eyes showed from behind all the hospital scrubs, but I knew it was Leonard.

Here I was, lying in an intensive care hospital room, my body covered with *staffococyl horriblus uncomfortabulus* (or something like that), about to lose my sanity, and in walks my best friend with lunch from Burger King. That was Leonard. He would do anything for me.

I had smashed my hand the summer after I graduated from high school and a virus had infected the cut and spread boils all over me. (Boils are like huge zits that hurt to touch and grow everywhere on your body.) They had to isolate me so I wouldn't infect anyone else.

The nurses strictly limited visitors to my immediate family, but Leonard . . . well, let's just say that somehow he had persuaded them to include him in that category. Every day Leonard would rush over from his summer job to the hospital to deliver another hamburger. He would visit again with my parents every evening and bring more real food.

A few days after my bout with jungle rot ended, Leonard and I left for different colleges. We've spent more than a decade apart since our high school days, but we're just as close as ever. Leonard is a friend.

Everyone needs at least one friend like Leonard, but not many people have that kind of sincere, lasting friendship.

The 4,000-Year-Old Friendship

My favorite story about friendship involves two men who went to war together, escaped from a manhunt and eventually ran a country. They both displayed great courage, intelligence and resourcefulness. They fought against huge odds and won. These two defended one another against all kinds of enemies.

Sounds like a good movie or novel, doesn't it? Their names were Jonathan and David. Their incredible, and true, story is found in the Bible.

To appreciate the depth of Jonathan and David's friendship you need to know about them as individuals. Let's check out Jonathan first.

A Man of Wealth

Jonathan was the oldest son of Saul, the king of Israel, and next in line for the throne.

Because of his position in life, how do you think Jonathan was treated? (To help you start writing, think how Donald Trump's children would be treated in your school.)

_____

_____

A Man of Character

History remembers the winners and the warriors. Jonathan definitely stands out as a man of great courage. Read 1 Samuel 13:1-7 and 14:1-23 for his report card.

What were the odds?

Philistines (see 13:5) _____   Israel (and 13:2) _____

At this point I would have been scared twist-legged. What about you? What would you do?

- Run with the guys across the Jordan?
- Hide in the nearest cave, thicket, rock, pit or cistern with the others?
- Stay safe near Saul?
- Take it to those Philistines?

What did Jonathan do? What happened? (Reread 1 Samuel 14:6-23.)

_____

_____

Pretty gutsy, right?

Now what kind of person do you think Jonathan was?

_____

_____

Dead-Eye David

You've probably heard a lot more about David than you have about Jonathan. David is one of the most famous people in all the Bible, but he didn't start that way. Read 1 Samuel 16:4-11 for a look at him growing up.

A Shepherd Boy

David was the baby of the family, the youngest of eight brothers. (Imagine how much he got picked on.) He got stuck with the worst job: tending the sheep. You can imagine each brother, as soon as he got old enough, pushing off the duty onto his younger brother. Only David didn't have anyone to push it off on.

When was the last time you were given a lousy job, the very worst one? How did you respond? Be honest!

_____

_____

_____

When Samuel came to look over Jesse's sons, they didn't even think about David. He was left out again. That tells a lot about how his brothers treated him.

A Real "Swinger"

You saw earlier that Jonathan was a courageous warrior. What about David? Read 1 Samuel 17. Everyone has *heard* the story of David and Goliath, but this may be the first time you've ever *read* it.

What would you estimate were David's chances of winning?

_____ to _____

In facing Goliath, David sure wasn't encouraged by the others very much. Look at what his brother said in verse 28. If that's not bad enough, the king said, "You are not able to fight him; you are only a boy."

David probably thought, "Thanks a lot!"

First, think about how would you have felt in David's place, then write down how you would have responded differently from David.

How I would feel   **What I would have done**

_____   _____

_____   _____

This wasn't the first time David had faced overwhelming odds. What had happened earlier? (1 Samuel 17:34-36)

_____

_____

Getting Off the Track

If David was so confident, why do you think he chose five stones (1 Samuel 17:40) and not just one as he left to fight Goliath?

_____

_____

(For the answer, turn to the end of the chapter.)

What do you think of David now?

_____

_____

You begin to see what kind of person David was. Given the most degrading job, he had done the very best work. He was picked on, taken for granted, forgotten about, cut down and everything else that can happen to the baby brother in a family of eight guys, but he confidently trusted God.

In what ways were Jonathan and David different?

David　　　　　　　　　　**Jonathan**

_____　　　　_____

_____   _____

_____   _____

In what ways were they alike?

David   **Jonathan**

_____   _____

_____   _____

_____   _____

Nothing to Gain, Everything to Lose

Now that you know Jonathan and David better you may wonder, *How on earth did these two guys get to be best friends?* It sure puzzles me. I can figure out more reasons why they *wouldn't* have been friends:

Too Cool

Both of these guys were battle-hardened fighters. They were as tough as Clint Eastwood and John Wayne put together. Generally speaking, most tough guys like these two don't want to depend on anyone else. They're too proud for that, so they don't make close friendships.

Too Mature

If Jonathan wasn't older than David, he was definitely more mature and experienced. By the time David stepped on the scene, Jonathan had been kicking Philistines around for quite some time. Rarely do big-time seniors become friends with a lowly freshman. It's beneath their "dignity."

Too Rich

Jonathan was a prince, David a shepherd boy. Jonathan had responsibility for a thousand men, David for a few sheep. They came from different worlds. How often does the school's rich kid befriend the poor kid in town?

Too Competitive

The biggest reason I think Jonathan and David would not have been friends was their competition for the throne. Jonathan was heir to the throne by birth, but David was the anointed one for the job (1 Samuel 16:13). And Jonathan knew it! (1 Samuel 23:17) That's like two friends both running for class president.

All this points out an important principle of making friends:

> Pride, status, wealth and competition
> can keep you from making the best of friends.

Jonathan had nothing to gain but everything to lose in becoming David's best friend. Yet he risked it all.

The Friendship Payoff

From all outward appearances, David had nothing that would profit Jonathan. Why, then, would Jonathan risk his pride, his wealth and status, even his right to the throne to make friends with David? Because David offered something better. David offered the best friendship a guy could ever have, so Jonathan's risk paid off big time. Here's how:

Faith

David and Jonathan shared an unswerving, unshakable faith in God. Until you've made a close Christian friend, you really can't understand the depth that this adds to the relationship. The spiritual dimension bonds you to the other person.

Trust

Each of these men, more than once, trusted the other with his life.

Loyalty

David and Jonathan wouldn't betray each other for anyone or anything. They were as loyal to one another as they were to God.

Love

You can imagine how all these qualities together caused their love for each other to grow and grow and grow. They loved each other better than life itself.

David couldn't offer gifts, vacations at the beach or connections to influential people. But he did offer what really counts in a relationship: faith, trust, loyalty and love. These qualities enabled David and Jonathan to become the closest of friends. To understand their friendship, read 1 Samuel 18:1, 18:3, 20:17. Who do you love like this? Who loves you like this?

_____

_____

Friends, best friends, are extremely valuable because of what they offer. To *gain* friends, you have to follow Jonathan's example.

> To experience friendship you must take the risk
> of offering your friendship first.

Don't be like most people who want someone to reach out to them first. Be daring: Take the risk and be the first to reach out. Sounds too hard? Keep reading.

Making Friends With David

"The soul of Jonathan was knit to the soul of David" (1 Samuel 18:1). That is what a best friend is all about: two people who are tight, real tight. To build friendships like this, follow the same path that Jonathan took.

First, he **overlooked differences.** Every time you meet someone, ask yourself if you might become the best of friends with this person. You never know when God might bring a "David" across your path. Don't let pride, status, wealth or competition fake you out of a new friend.

Second, Jonathan **risked it.** Don't wait on the other person to reach out to you first. Most people let thoughts like, *I wonder what they will think of me?* and *What if they don't like me?* keep them from meeting new friends. Best friends have so much to offer. Take the risk.

The third step to having friends like David is to **be a friend first.**

```
To have a friend you must be a friend.
```

Friendship Factors

What kind of friend was Jonathan?

He Loved Unconditionally

Jonathan loved David as himself. This kind of love puts the other person first. How does a friend put this into practice? Read 1 Corinthians 13:4-8 and Philippians 2:3,4 for ideas. Write down four ways here.

_____   _____

_____   _____

He Learned to Listen

Jonathan listened when David talked with him. To become friends you must get to know each other. Asking questions is a great way to get to know your friend. Be sure to listen carefully to his answers. If you have trouble carrying on conversations, consider asking your friends questions like the ones below. The first letters in each category form the acrostic "FRIENDSHIP."[1]

Faith
- How did you become a Christian? When?
- Who in the Bible do you like the most? Why?

Reason
- What goals do you have?
- What is your purpose in life?

Involvements
- What extracurricular activities are you involved in?
- What do you do at your job?

Experiences
- What is Christmas like at your house?
- How have you spent your summers?

Needs
- How can I help you?
- What can I do for you?

Dreams
- Would you like to be a millionaire? Why or why not?
- What kind of impact would you like to have on the world?

School
- Which is your favorite class? Least favorite? Why?
- Do you think you will use what you are learning?

Home
- What do you like best about your parents?
- What is it like being the oldest? youngest? only child?

Interests
- What hobbies do you have?
- Who is your favorite music group? Why?

Prayer Requests
- How can I pray for you?
- What do you pray for yourself?

He Served Others

Jonathan told David, "Whatever you say I will do for

you." He made himself available to meet any and every one of David's needs.

He Stood Up for Those He Loved

Jonathan had it tough: His dad was after his best friend. Jonathan had to stick up for David without being disloyal to his father. That can be a trick, but Jonathan did it. Several times he protected David from his father, but Jonathan proved his loyalty to his father by dying beside him on the battlefield (2 Samuel 2:4).

Your friend's reputation may come under attack. Joining in the attack or staying silent are the easy ways out. If your friend's reputation is being put down, try your best to protect your friend without turning against the attacker.

Think about last week. How did you do at standing up for your friends? Did you initiate the cut downs and attacks? Did you join in? Did you stay silent?

_____

_____

He Hurt When Others Hurt

Jonathan grieved over his father wanting to have David killed. He hurt on the inside because he knew David hurt on the inside. To build a closer friendship, help shoulder the burdens and difficulties that come your friend's way. Whenever your friend experiences problems at home or at school, make yourself available. Just being there is often enough.

Have you ever been in a really tough situation? How would you feel if someone like Jonathan befriended you?

_____

_____

He Understood Feelings

How often do you see the school's two biggest jocks hugging each other in the hall and kissing each other in the midst of tears? Probably not very often, yet Jonathan and David did just that. They freely expressed their feelings for one another because they knew that the other understood.

He Was Totally Committed

It's easy to give up on people. Friends will hurt you, reject you and let you down. But even in the worst of it, hang tough. Be a true friend. Commit yourself to the other person in such a way that your friendship stands the test of time, distance and even hurt. Jonathan and David shared a friendship that lasted a lifetime.

By now you can see that Jonathan and David illustrate perfectly what best friends offer each other. Read the verses and match them with the correct friendship factor. (Check your answers with the key at the end of the chapter.)

A best friend will . . .

____ 1. Love you even when you are unlovable.

____ 2. Speak positively about you when others don't.

____ 3. Listen to your problems.

____ 4. Do anything for you, regardless of the inconvenience.

____ 5. Always protect you from the bad guys

____ 6. Hurt when you hurt.

____ 7. Understand your deepest feelings.

____ 8. Be committed to you.

Scripture

A. 1 Samuel 20:19

B. 1 Samuel 20:4

C. 1 Samuel 20:42

D. 1 Samuel 20:1,2

E. 1 Samuel 20:17

F. 1 Samuel 19:4

G. 1 Samuel 20:41

H. 1 Samuel 20:34

Friends Under Construction

Remember the principles? To make close friendships you must:

1. Avoid pride, status, wealth and competition.

2. Reach out first.

3. Be a friend to have a friend.

One last principle. Making tight friends for some people is easy, but for most of us, making close friendships takes lots of work.

> Work hard at making friends.

Don't give up if you don't make close friends right away. Keep trying, it's worth it.

Oh, by the way, Leonard and I are getting together for lunch next week. I can't wait.

Making the Best of Them

As you answer these questions, be completely honest with yourself. The better you understand yourself, the better friend you'll be.

1. What hinders you from making more friends? Tell how.

Pride _____

Money _____

Status _____

Competition_____

2. Do you usually reach out first or wait for the other person to initiate the friendship? Try to explain why and give

an example.

_____

_____

_____

3. Which of the eight friendship factors (p. 18) do you need to work on the most? What will you do to work on it?

Factor: _____

Action: _____

_____

_____

Memorize Proverbs 17:17

Answer Key

Getting Off Track: David collected five stones because Goliath had four brothers (1 Chronicles 20:4-8; 2 Samuel 21:18-22). David wasn't just confident, he was super-confident. He knew for sure that he could hit a nine-foot target, right between the eyes, five times in a row.

Friendship Factors: 1. E, 2. F, 3. D, 4. B, 5. A, 6. H, 7. G, 8. C.

---

1. Adapted from *Love: Making it Last* by Barry St. Clair and Bill Jones (San Bernardino, CA: Here's Life Publishers, 1988), pp. 67-69. Used by permission.

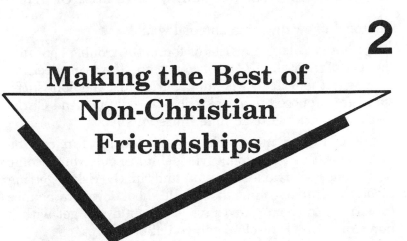

Making the Best of Non-Christian Friendships

Lying on the floor in the backseat of a car, figuring I was about to be arrested or die, I thought, *This is fun?*

My friends had found a water-loaded fire extinguisher just lying around (sure!) and thought it'd be fun to drive into town and spray people. At first I had refused, but since I hadn't made many friends yet (I was a lowly college freshman) and I was lonely, I let them persuade me.

After we drenched the first two people, I stopped laughing. I felt sorry for those people, standing there dripping wet. We shot a few more, then pulled up to a dark corner and blasted a guy. As he turned around, his dark clothes turned into a policeman's uniform, complete with gun, badge and handcuffs. He was furious.

He ran to his car to chase us down, but my friends sped away.

I thought they were crazy. How could my friends imagine that we could get away? Even if the policeman didn't catch us now, he had our license plate number and a description of our car. He would get us sooner or later, and trying to get away would only make things worse. I was so scared I got down on the floor of the car. If the police didn't kill me, I knew my mom and dad would!

Should I blame my friends for all the trouble I got into because of their "fun"? No, of course not. It was my decision to go with them. They were non-Christians, and non-Christians are supposed to act like non-Christians. (And Christians are supposed to act like Christians.)

Turning to non-Christian friends for fun can be dangerous. But what about friendship? Should you become best friends with non-Christians and run the risk of getting involved in fun like mine that would shoot down any chance to witness to them? How involved should you get with a non-Christian? How close can you afford to get?

These are questions you've probably asked yourself without knowing how to find the answers. For some help, consider the story of Samson and Delilah.

Strong But Not Invincible

You probably already know Samson was the strongest man who ever lived. But Samson was a lot more than a bunch of muscles strung together. Read Judges 13 – 16 for a better picture of him. From these chapters you find that Samson had:

A Great Family

What were Samson's parents like? Describe what you think of them (see Judges 13).

_____

_____

A Great Purpose

What purpose did the Lord have for Samson's life? (Judges 13:5)

_____

_____

After Moses and Joshua died, no one leader could guide Israel with the faith and wisdom these men displayed, so the nation entered a period of time characterized mainly by rebellion against God and slavery to other nations. God had picked Samson to deliver Israel from all of this.

A Great Relationship With God

According to Judges 13:24, what was God's attitude toward Samson? What was Samson's attitude toward God? (Hebrews 11:32-34)

_____

_____

A Great Power

Samson is called the strongest man who ever lived. How was this strength displayed in these passages and what was its ultimate source?

Judges 14:5,6 _____

Judges 15:13-15 _____

Samson seems to be a man who had everything going for him. He had a great family, purpose, relationship with God and power.

A Great Weakness

But Samson also had a great weakness. He was easily influenced. He tended to give in to the pressures of his unbelieving friends. You find the classic example of Samson's weakness in Judges 16:4-21, where the famous story of Samson and Delilah is told. As you fill in the chart below, notice how Samson gives in a little more during each confrontation with Delilah, his nonbelieving "friend."

	4-9	10-12	13-14	15-21
Delilah's Request				
Samson's Response				
Result				

A Great Downfall

Even though Samson had so much going for him, he suffered great loss because he allowed an unbeliever to influence him. Not only did Samson lose his strength, but he also lost his anointing, his eyesight, his freedom, his honor and eventually his life.

Did all this have to happen? No! The lesson from Samson's story seems obvious: Never build close friendships with non-Christians.

Who's Influencing Who?

What do you think? Should a Christian have close friendships with a non-Christian? Could anything good ever come out of that kind of relationship?

The best way to answer these questions (and most others) is to look at the life of Jesus and ask, "What would He have done?" Matthew 11:19 says He was "a friend of tax-gatherers and sinners." According to this, then, the answer is *yes,* Christians should be friends with non-Christians. Talk about something good happening. What could be better than your friends coming to Christ?

But you say, "What about Samson?" Good point. The key word when it comes to making the best of a non-Christian friendship is *influence.* If you have a friendship with a non-Christian, the first question you must ask yourself is, "Who is influencing who?"

Think back to the beginning of this chapter. My unbelieving friends were influencing me, and the result was big trouble. (I'm still on parole.) Samson, too, fell under the influence of non-Christian friends, and it cost him his life.

This happened to a friend of mine from high school. Although we went to different high schools, we were great friends. We knew each other through wrestling. Because we weighed the same, we often competed against one another in tournaments. Neither team could understand us. We would laugh and joke around, and show each other new wrestling moves right until the time we wrestled each other. I cared for him a lot. We were close.

But he had two problems. First, he always beat me when we wrestled each other. (Would you believe I let him win?) Second, he always let others influence him. I lost touch with him after college, but I heard about him a few years later. He was found, all 100 pounds of him, in a dumpster where his druggie friends left him for dead.

When a non-Christian influences you,
you're headed for trouble.
When you influence your non-Christian friend,
you make the best of the friendship.

Many Christians join the battle for the souls of their

non-Christian friends only to be taken captive. They begin by reaching out and end up compromising. They start out influencing and finish being influenced. How can you avoid this same problem? Let's go back and look at Samson's mistakes.

Guard Your Weaknesses

Samson was easily influenced by Delilah because he left one of his weaknesses, his lust, unguarded. Samson had a history of letting his lust get in the way. Read the following verses, identify the woman and write down whether or not the relationship honored God.

Passage	Further Insight	Woman	Honored God?
Judges 14:1-4	Deut. 7:3,4	_____	_____
Judges 16:1	Exodus 20:14	_____	_____
Judges 16:4	Joshua 23:11-13	_____	_____

Because of his past, Samson should never have begun a friendship with Delilah. (He would have been much safer reaching out to the weight lifters.) He knew he was too weak in the area of lust, yet he hung around Delilah anyway and she influenced Samson to compromise.

You may have a weakness in a certain area—lust, drugs, drinking, stealing, rebellion, lying. Be on guard. Keep yourself out of tempting situations altogether. Let's say you're a former drug user. It's true you'd probably relate better to a non-Christian druggie than anyone else, but it would be suicide to go into a drug environment if you are still tempted by drugs. How much better to reach out to other non-Christians until you are strong enough to resist temptation.

What about your friendships with non-Christians right now? Are you pulling them up toward Christ or are they pulling you down in your area of weakness? Write down your three closest non-Christian friends and evaluate who is influencing who.

Friend	How I'm influencing them	How they are influencing me
1.		
2.		
3.		

> To make the best of a non-Christian friendship, regularly evaluate who is influencing who.

Fill out the chart above on a regular basis. What difference do you think it would have made in Samson's life if he would have reviewed this chart?

_____

_____

Now that you have seriously thought about your non-Christian friends, you may have some questions. If they are influencing you, you may ask, "What can I do to keep from being influenced?" If you are influencing them, you may wonder, "How can I lead them to Christ?" Let's consider first what to do if your non-Christian friends are influencing you.

The Great Escape

If you compromise in the process of reaching out to

non-Christians, you can do more harm than good. There are dozens of ways non-Christians can influence you. Second Timothy 3:2-4 names a few. List some of them:

_____   _____

_____   _____

_____   _____

How does verse five say to respond?

_____

_____

In order to make the best of a non-Christian friendship in which you are being influenced, you must break it off. This is rarely easy.

I can remember when I first became a Christian, I had to back off of a lot of friendships because I kept giving in to their persuasive words and getting into a lot of trouble. As a result I spent many lonely nights in my dorm room. Initially it was hard, very hard, but after a few months it paid off. First, I grew in my relationship with Christ. In my loneliness, He became my best friend. Second, I met a lot of strong Christians who became my closest friends. Third, I became strong enough to go back and influence my old friends toward Christ.

What are the advantages and disadvantages of staying with a non-Christian friend who is influencing you?

Advantages   **Disadvantages**

_____   _____

_____   _____

_____   _____

What are the advantages and disadvantages of backing off?

Advantages   **Disadvantages**

_____   _____

_____   _____

_____   _____

If you back off a friendship with a non-Christian, you will want to tell him or her why. Here's what you might say, "You know, Delilah, I've renewed my commitment to Jesus Christ and I don't want to disappoint Him anymore by doing the things I've been doing lately. If you want to do those things without me that's up to you, but I don't want to join you anymore. If you would like to get closer to the Lord with me that would be great! What do you think?"

This is just a suggestion. You put it in your own words. Just keep in mind these pointers:

- Identify yourself with Christ.
- Display humility, not a holier-than-thou attitude.
- Be gentle in your conversation, yet firm in your decision.
- Invite him or her to join you in getting closer to Christ.

Remember, it will be tough to back off, but continuing to compromise will be tougher, especially in the long run.

Party Time

Do you know many "partiers"? I mean the big-time, blowout kind of partiers? The partyingest bunch of people I've ever heard of are in heaven. That's right—heaven, not hell. Listen to what Luke 15:7 says: "There will be more joy in heaven over one sinner who repents . . . " Heaven has one big time blowout every time a person comes to Christ.

Have you hosted any of those parties lately? Have you had the opportunity of leading one of your friends to Christ? If you would like to see your friends come to know Christ, follow these party prep steps.

Pray for Your Friends

Ask God to convict your friends of sin, righteousness and judgment (John 16:8-11). Ask Him to lead them to the knowledge of the truth so they would come to their senses and escape from the snare of the devil, having been held captive by him to do his will (2 Timothy 2:25,26). Ask God to enable you to share the gospel with boldness (Ephesians 6:19).

Share the Good News

The first opportunity you get, tell your friends the Good News of the gospel. The Good News has four parts:

- God loves them.
- Their disobedience separates them from God.
- Their disobedience must be punished.
- Jesus Christ was punished on their behalf.

Invite Them to Respond

Let your friends know it's not enough just to hear about the Good News. It only becomes theirs when, by faith, they ask Christ to be their Lord and Savior. So after you share the Good News, ask them if they would like to commit themselves to Christ.

Followup Regardless of the Response

If they accept the Good News, you will want to get your friends plugged in to a church right away. You will also want to teach them how to grow in their faith. A good place to begin with is this book. Share with them the importance of friendships.

If they reject the Good News, don't give up. Continue to pray for your friends, love them and tell them about the importance of coming to Christ.

Remember the Rewards, But Don't Forget the Risks

No greater joy exists than seeing your non-Christian friends come to Christ. But be careful that in reaching out to them you don't give in to them. Know your weaknesses and always guard them. Like Samson, if you aren't careful you can bring yourself and the cause of Christ a lot of harm. Making it a practice to regularly evaluate your friendships can keep you out of trouble. Remember, *influence* is the key word.

Making the Best of Them

1. In what areas are you easily pulled down in your walk with Christ?

_____

_____

_____

2. How well do you guard yourself in these areas?

_____

_____

_____

3. Who are your non-Christian friends?

_____

_____

_____

4. Pick a non-Christian friend who you are influencing toward Christ. Write your plan to share the Good News with him:

_____

_____

_____

5. Pick a non-Christian friend who's the worst influence on you. Write your plan to back off in your friendship. How can you be praying for this friendship?

_____

_____

_____

Memorize 1 Corinthians 15:33

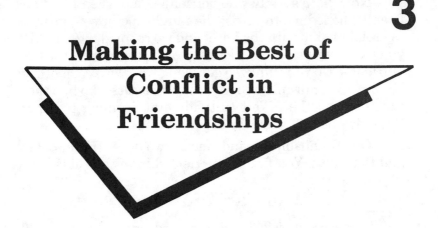

Making the Best of Conflict in Friendships

3

After four hours of studying for a chemistry test, my brain had cooked, fried and evaporated. Only my stomach was functioning now, and it was screaming for peanut butter and honey sandwiches.

Before leaving the library, I stopped to talk with some of the guys in my chemistry class. I had hoped to pick up a few more pointers for the test the next day, or at least they might have some food. They didn't have either, so I left.

The next morning one of the guys from that table sat down beside me. His name was David. I later found out he was a genius. (I wasn't.) He was also a Christian. (I wasn't one of those either.) After the test we had lunch together. We hit it off as friends, so he began dropping by my dorm room, inviting me to eat, play ball and study. As we spent time together he often told me about my need for Christ. It wasn't long before I invited Christ into my heart. (I'm still trying to figure out how to become a genius, though.)

The next quarter David and I became roommates. Morning after morning I watched him read his Bible and pray. I soon started doing the same. He really helped me grow in my faith.

Now, here's a guy who befriended me when I had few friends; he led me to Christ; he taught me how to grow in my relationship with the Lord; and we roomed together. Do you think we were close friends? You bet we were—the best of friends. Do you think we got along well with each other? No way. After awhile we fought like two cats who had their tails tied together. We eventually quit rooming together. Yet today he and I remain best of friends.

Our friendship reminds me of two other friends, Paul and Barnabas. You find their friendship in the Bible.

Who Can You Trust?

The woman kicked and screamed, crying for her child, as the religious zealot carried her off. Her captor threatened to have her murdered but settled for throwing her into prison. Her crime: proclaiming "Jesus is Lord."

Her captor had received permission to carry on his work in Damascus. The next morning he would be off on his mission.

News of his coming raced ahead of him. Terrified, the Christians prepared for his coming. And waited.

As Saul neared Damascus on his journey, a light from heaven suddenly flashed around him. He fell to the ground and heard a voice say to him, "Saul, Saul, why do you persecute me?"

"Who are you, Lord?" Saul asked.

"I am Jesus, whom you are persecuting," He replied. "Now get up and go into the city, and you will be told what you must do."

Saul got up from the ground, but when he opened his eyes he couldn't see anything. So his fellow travelers led him by the hand into Damascus.

In Damascus, a Christian prayed for Saul (renamed

Paul by the Lord). Immediately Paul regained his eyesight and not long afterward he began to preach about Christ.

Talk about confusing. The Christians couldn't get over it, and the Jews were infuriated.

To the Jews, Paul was a traitor of the worst kind. They began plotting how to do away with him.

To the Christians, he was a man with a history of deception, treachery and cruelty. Was his "conversion" all a trick to lure them into some trap to destroy them all?

Everyone stayed away from him.

Enter Barnabas

Barnabas didn't understand what drew him to Paul. Taking a big chance, Barnabas asked Paul to meet him at the McHerod's on Solomon Street. Over a Jonah Jumbo sandwich they talked.

When they finished, Barnabas thought, *This guy is right on target! He really has changed. He is a believer. Wait till Pete and the guys hear about this!*

Later that afternoon Barnabas convinced the other disciples that Paul was for real.

The Acts of the Apostles

In the months that followed, Paul and Barnabas began to travel together. As a ministry team, they had all kinds of exciting experiences together. Here are just a few.

They Curse a Magician (Acts 13:6-12)

When Paul and Barnabas taught a government official about Jesus, a magician tried to oppose them. Bad move. Paul stared at the magician and declared, "You are a child of the devil and an enemy of everything that is right. You are full of all kinds of deceit and trickery. Will you never stop perverting the right ways of the Lord?" If that wasn't enough, he prayed that the magician would lose his eyesight, and he did! (By the way, the official believed in Christ as a result of Paul's witness.)

Have you and a friend ever prayed a big prayer that God answered quickly? What did this do to your friendship?

_____

_____

They Heal a Lame Man (Acts 14:8-18)

On another occasion Paul was preaching when he noticed a man who had been lame since birth. Right in the middle of his speech Paul looked at the lame man and commanded him to walk. (Wonder what Barnabas must have been thinking!) Immediately the man jumped up and began to walk! The people standing by went nuts.

Have you and a friend ever done something really successful or popular? How did it make you feel toward one another?

_____

_____

They Lead People to Christ (Acts 13:44-49)

Paul and Barnabas grew to be tight friends because they had the same purpose in life: They wanted to lead people to Christ. And they did! Lots of people.

Have you ever led someone to Christ with a friend? Describe the first time and your memory of it. How did it make you feel toward one another?

_____

_____

They Experience Persecution

During their travels, Paul and Barnabas had many exciting times, but they went through tough times together as well. To say that not everyone got excited about the work they performed in Christ's name is putting it mildly. The Jews hated these guys and tried on several occasions to kill them. What do the following verses say about this?

Acts 13:50 _____

Acts 14:2-7 _____

Acts 14:19,20 _____

Imagine yourself holding your friend in your arms after the Jews had dragged him out of the city and stoned him. He is covered with bruises and bleeding all over. Everyone supposes he is dead. Then he looks up at you, winks and says, "Let's go back into the city. I wasn't finished preaching. I have one more point in my sermon to make."

Have you and a friend ever been made fun of because you were Christians? How did it affect your friendship?

_____

_____

The Spats of the Apostles

Two friends who had traveled together, ministered together and been persecuted together should never have any spats, right? Wrong. At least not these two. They had a big blowup. Read about it in Acts 15:36-40.

Paul and Barnabas had returned home from their travels, but they couldn't sit still for long. They wanted to go on a second ministry trip. One snag, though. Barnabas wanted to take John Mark with them. Paul didn't. Paul said that the wimp had deserted them on the first trip (Acts 13:13) and he wouldn't have the kid do it again. Paul and Barnabas got so upset with each other over this that they split up.

These two men were very godly, very tight, but very stubborn.

Why do you think Barnabas insisted on taking John Mark along?

_____

_____

Why do you think Paul insisted on leaving him behind?

_____

_____

Who do you think was right, Barnabas or Paul? Why?

_____

_____

Paul and Barnabas's friendship illustrates an important truth.

Conflict with friends is inevitable.

Regardless of how close you are as friends, sooner or later you will have a fight. It happens every time.

Major Misunderstanding

Paul and Barnabas did not start out that day planning to have a fight. Paul did not wake up and say, "I'm in a bad mood. If any one crosses me today I'm going to snatch him bald-headed." Nor did Barnabas plot the night before how he could be a royal pain in the neck to Paul. Neither wanted to fight. They were the best of friends. It just happened.

Why? Because of a major misunderstanding. They saw the situation (taking John Mark along) from two completely different perspectives. Paul, a "project person," saw John Mark as a liability to what he wanted to accomplish. The deserter might slow them down. John Mark's lack of faith, courage and perseverance might discourage the rest of the team. To Paul, the most important issue was accomplishing the goal.

Barnabas, a "people person," saw the situation differently. He knew how John Mark felt, a young man who had failed in his first big venture. Every time John Mark walked into church, people would begin to whisper, "There's the guy who chickened out on Paul and Barnabas. Left them high and dry, he did." Barnabas wanted to give John Mark another chance, an opportunity to prove himself, regain his confidence, put the past behind him. Barnabas cared for the individual and wanted the best for John Mark. To Barnabas, the important issue was realizing the future potential of the person.

Who was right, Paul or Barnabas? They both were— sort of.

You see, it was God who made Paul a "project person." Without folks like Paul the early church would not have grown like it did. He had a goal: to preach the gospel to all creation.

God also made Barnabas a "people person." Without Barnabas, folks like Paul would never have been given a chance. (Remember, everyone was afraid of Paul until Barnabas reached out, befriended him and convinced the Christians of Paul's sincerity.)

God makes both the "project person" and the "people

person." Why? Because both are needed.

Conflict results between close friends when they fail to understand and appreciate the personality that God has given to each of them.

> Lack of understanding is a major cause of conflict between close friends.

Though conflict is inevitable, it doesn't have to break up a friendship like it did with Paul and Barnabas. You can use conflict to help your friendship to grow.

In order to make the best of conflict between you and a close friend of yours, follow these three guidelines:

- Understand your personality differences.
- Strengthen your personality weaknesses.
- Fight by the rules.

Understand Personality Differences

From Paul and Barnabas's relationship you learned that God gives different people different personalities or temperaments. What are these personalities and how do they work?

Hippocrates, a man who lived centuries before the birth of Christ, noticed the similarities in certain people. As a result he divided people into four groups according to their temperaments: sanguine, choleric, melancholy and phlegmatic. These terms and groups are still helpful to classify general personality types. Understanding the differences between these temperaments will enable you to better handle conflict when it arises.

The following list contains a few characteristics of each temperament. Go through and check one characteristic from each row that best describes you. You'll have a total of ten checks when you're through.[1]

Sanguine	Choleric	Melancholy	Phlegmatic
1. ☐ Playful	☐ Persuasive	☐ Persistent	☐ Peaceful
2. ☐ Sociable	☐ Strong-willed	☐ Self-sacrificing	☐ Submissive
3. ☐ Optimistic	☐ Outspoken	☐ Orderly	☐ Obliging
4. ☐ Funny	☐ Forceful	☐ Faithful	☐ Friendly
5. ☐ Lively	☐ Leader	☐ Loyal	☐ Listener
6. ☐ Undisciplined	☐ Unsympathetic	☐ Unforgiving	☐ Unenthusiastic
7. ☐ Forgetful	☐ Frank	☐ Fussy	☐ Fearful
8. ☐ Interrupts	☐ Impatient	☐ Insecure	☐ Indecisive
9. ☐ Unpredictable	☐ Unaffectionate	☐ Unpopular	☐ Uninvolved
10. ☐ Haphazard	☐ Headstrong	☐ Hard-to-please	☐ Hesitant

You probably discovered that although you didn't mark all the characteristics under one column, you did find yourself more one personality type than the other three. Keep in mind that no one personality type is better than another, just different.

In general, what do you like most about other people?

_____

_____

What irritates you most about other people?

_____

_____

Each personality type offers its own strengths, but it also has its own weaknesses that can create conflict with people of other types. For example, a sanguine talks easily with others (strength), but at times they can talk you to death (weakness). A choleric loves getting jobs done (strength), but tends to be insensitive to the needs of others (weakness). A melancholy is very thorough (strength), but can become too picky (weakness). A phlegmatic rarely gets uptight (strength), but can become lazy (weakness).

From what you know of temperaments now, what temperaments do you think Paul and Barnabas had?

Paul: _____ Barnabas: _____

Why did these men need each other?_____

_____

Learn to recognize the strengths and weaknesses of both yours and your friend's temperament. Think through which characteristics of your temperament might tend to irritate your friend and be sensitive to them. Also think about which characteristics of your friend's temperament will irritate you and learn to be patient. To help you, fill out the following chart:

Temperament

My primary temperament: _____

My friend's temperament: _____

Strengths

My strengths	My friend's strengths
_____	_____
_____	_____
_____	_____

Weaknesses

My weaknesses	My friend's weaknesses
_____	_____
_____	_____
_____	_____

Potential Conflict

I tend to irritate my friend by _____

_____

My friend tends to irritate me by _____

_____

What we will do to minimize the conflict: _____

_____

Understanding the differences in temperaments is the first step to making the best of conflict, but, unfortunately, it doesn't solve all your problems. Read on.

Strengthening Your Personality Weaknesses

I've been told all my life how insensitive I am. One time a friend of mine told me his girlfriend just broke up with him (they were real tight), and I responded: "No big deal. There are plenty of girls out there, and you can do a lot better than her anyway."

I was *trying* to comfort and encourage him. Instead, I crushed him.

Now that wasn't my fault, was it? After all, I'm a choleric. Cholerics aren't supposed to be sensitive. That's the way God made me, isn't it?

Just because God gave me a certain personality doesn't mean I can't change. We're *all* expected to change and adapt. It's a cop-out to blame fights with your friends on your personality by saying, "That's just the way I am."

Paul and Barnabas probably responded like that. Perhaps you and a friend have found yourself in that type of situation before. If so, you need to work on diminishing your weaknesses and developing your strengths. You need to learn how to respond like Jesus.

What personality type do you think Jesus was? When you read passages like casting the money changers out of the temple, you think he was choleric. But when you read about how he laid his life down for his friends, you may think he was a melancholy. What about Jesus making friends so easily with tax-gatherers and sinners? Sanguine. Or how he never was in a hurry? Phlegmatic.

Jesus' personality combined all the strengths of all the temperaments yet included none of the weaknesses.

You can have the same personality — as you allow the Holy Spirit to fill you with the qualities that Jesus had. What kind of qualities does the Holy Spirit build into your life? Read Galatians 5:22,23 and write them down.

_____

_____

How would you like a personality like that? *Me? Live like this?* you may be thinking. Absolutely! In fact, it's what God is planning for you. When you became a Christian, the Holy Spirit came to live inside of you. He came for a specific purpose: to enable you to be and act like Jesus. He wants to live His life through you!

Two things have to happen for the Holy Spirit to effectively work in your life:

Confess every sin to God. Sin blocks the Holy Spirit's power in you. To deal with your sin, tell God about it, down to the last detail. Be honest. Tell Him how wrong it was, and accept your part in it. Don't blame anyone else. Tell him how sorry you are. Then ask Him to forgive you.

Ask the Lord to control you. Tell the Lord you want Him to fill you with His personality, to enable you to be and act like Jesus.

When you follow this two-step process, you are no longer at the mercy of the negatives of your old personality. You overcome the weaknesses of your personality and become a much better friend. Not only that, you can now really accept the frustrating habits of your close friends. With the Holy Spirit's power you can display "patience" and "kindness" (instead of fighting) when your friends do something to irritate you.

What changes would the Holy Spirit's power have made in Paul and Barnabas's situation concerning John Mark?

_____

_____

Think of the last conflict you had with one of your friends. What difference would the Spirit's control have made in that situation?

_____

_____

Fighting Fairly?

Think about that last fight again and how it ended up.

You won't always understand the difference in your personalities. Nor will you always allow the Holy Spirit to control you. So once you're in a fight, the issue becomes how to handle it. You can either fight dirty or fight fairly.[2]

Although you probably won't use a punch to get back at your friend, you can do just as much damage with your words and actions. Which of these dirty fighting tactics have you used?

Biting. You open your mouth and let your friend have it by criticizing (tell him how he did everything wrong), belittling (make fun of him) and humiliating (try to burn him in front of other people) him.

Kicking. When you kick someone, you want him to feel the pain. You tell your friend how he messed things up. You throw in a few comments like, "If only you had done things differently," or "I can't believe you did such a thing!"

Scratching. You scratch by interrupting, a great maneuver to distract your friend. You never let her finish saying anything to explain herself. You do all the talking.

Gouging the eyes. By blurring the issue you verbally blind your friend, using words like *always* and *never* to your advantage—"You *never* call me up. I *always* call you."

Pulling hair. When you pull someone's hair, you have him at your mercy. You do this effectively by yanking on his emotions. Yell, scream, utter threats, get red in the face. If he is slow to catch on, tell him you are MAD. If anger doesn't produce the desired effect, don't panic. Use silence.

Hitting below the belt. You reach a point sometime in the conflict when you must decide whether to let your friend suffer a little bit more (but live to see another day), or put him out of his misery permanently. When you choose to do the latter, you hit him where it hurts the most. You know his point of vulnerability and go for it, taking every cheap shot you can.

Which of these dirty tactics do you tend to use most often in fights with your friends?

_____

_____

Using these tactics almost guarantees that you'll come out of the fight the winner. However, in winning the fight you lose the war. When you have an attitude of "Win at any cost, even if I have to fight dirty," you ultimately lose the relationship—a high price to pay. If you consider the cost too high, then fight fair.

Fighting by the Rules

These rules will help keep the fight clean.

Desire openness. In a fair fight, the attitude of "I'm always right" is against the rules. Ask God to point out every area in your life where you are wrong. Confess anything the Lord shows you.

Choose the right timing. Arguments can break out at awkward times. To fight by the rules, wait until both of you can give the time and attention necessary to talk things out.

Select the right words. Think before you speak. To know the right words to say, you'll have to first listen to your friend when she speaks. Determine if your words will help or hinder in working out the problem.

Guard your tone of voice. You can say the right words the wrong way. If you project sarcasm or criticism in your voice, your friend will pick it up.

Look at the other person's point of view. While your friend talks, listen carefully to understand where he is coming from. In viewing the conflict, put yourself in his place. When you do this, think of how he feels instead of how you feel or why you think he was wrong.

Identify the problem. Discover the main issue that started the fight. It may be more than meets the eye. For example, she may have gotten upset because you said the wrong thing when actually she was already upset because the night before you spent time with another friend.

Determine the solution. Once you identify the problem, decide on a solution. Make the solution practical and realistic. Don't give up until you have worked things out satisfactorily. Talk about how to keep this conflict from happening again.

Confess any wrongdoing. During the fight if you discover you have hurt your friend, immediately ask forgiveness. Say, "I was wrong about _____. I can see how that hurt you. Will you forgive me?"

Forgive any wrongdoing. Your friend may have hurt you. If so, forgive him, even if he doesn't ask you to. If he doesn't ask, verbalize your forgiveness of him to the Lord alone in prayer.

Pray together. After the fight, pray together. Ask the Lord to let you learn from the conflict and grow closer together because of it. Ask Him to overcome the problem so you won't have to fight over this issue again.

Paul and Barnabas must have eventually handled their conflict by fighting by the rules. Even though they didn't go on the trip together, the story has a happy ending.

Paul had returned from his trip and had left on a third one. He was in prison alone, except for Luke. He knew he didn't have long to live. He wrote a letter to Timothy, asking him to come visit. As he closed the letter, Paul also asked for John Mark to come. And then he paid one of the highest compliments a choleric can pay by saying, "John Mark is useful to me for service."

Conflict is inevitable. How you handle it isn't. Fighting by the rules will help you make the best of friends even in conflict—like David and I have done.

Making the Best of Them

1. What did you learn about yourself and what kind of friend you are in this chapter?

_____

_____

2. How will understanding yours and your friend's temperaments help you avoid conflict?

_____

_____

_____

3. How will having the personality of Jesus expressed through your life by the Holy Spirit help you in your friendships?

_____

_____

_____

4. Think about your most recent conflict with a friend. In what ways did you fight dirty? What do you need to do about your friendship at this point?

_____

_____

_____

Memorize Proverbs 15:1

---

1. Adapted from "Personality Plus" by Fred and Florence Littauer (Redlands, CA). Used by permission.

2. Adapted from *Love: Making It Last* by Barry St. Clair and Bill Jones (San Bernardino, CA: Here's Life Publishers, 1988), pp. 90-95. Used by permission.

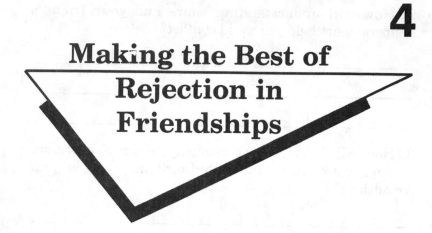

Making the Best of Rejection in Friendships

4

The laughs cut deeply, but I tried my hardest to act like it didn't bother me. I wanted to cry, to slam my locker (with their heads inside) and to run away . . . all at the same time. Instead, I just walked away, staring straight ahead, pretending I didn't hear them.

When I got home from school that afternoon I promised myself I would never go back. Later, after talking with one of my friends on the phone, I decided to go back just long enough to murder the three who had laughed at me. Then I would turn fugitive and hitchhike across the country, never to be seen or heard from again.

It all started because I had decided to run for a student government position against Gary. Gary's friends, who *used* to be my friends, were laughing and cutting me down. The campaign posters, though, went too far. Walking down the hall reading what they wrote made me feel like a jerk.

Having my friends turn on me like that brought some of the greatest pain I've ever known. I wished I could say it was the only time I've been through an experience like that, but it's not. Like me, you eventually have to face a fact of friendship:

> When you open yourself up to friendship, you also open yourself up to heartache.

I'm not sure I've ever met anyone who has *never* been rejected by one of his friends. It hurts bad, real bad.

The Unkindest Cut of All

Rejection. It's a word we all fear. Why? Because God has placed inside each one of us a desire to be loved by people, to be accepted. Nobody wants to be left out.

Rejection comes in many packages. Here are three of the most common:

- When your friends leave you out
- When your friends let you down
- When your friends laugh it up at your expense

Let's look at each one.

When Your Friends Leave You Out

You make your way through the maze of chairs and tables in the school cafeteria. You head toward "your" table, where you always sit with your friends. Trying not to spill your lunch (at least that's what the cafeteria staff calls it) on the cute girl's head beside you, you expertly balance your tray in one hand and pull your chair out with the other. You sit down just in time to hear, "So we'll meet at Toni's at 6:30 tonight."

"Where are we going?" you ask, completely unprepared for the deathly silence that follows.

Slowly and ever so meekly Toni, the cute girl beside you, says, "Well, my dad was able to get four tickets to the play-offs tonight. I didn't know you were here today . . .

Brad, Stephanie and Karl were here . . . I hope you understand."

Describe the most recent time you felt left out:

_____

_____

When Your Friends Let You Down

The telephone rings, interrupting your favorite TV show. You take the remote control and zap the volume down to a shouting level. You roll off the sofa and hustle over to the phone, desperately trying to swallow the last of the soft chocolate chip cookie you stuffed in your mouth the moment before the phone rang.

"Harro," you answer, embarrassed that your mouth is still full. It's Rich, your best friend, so you take another bite and say, "I can't wait to go camping this weekend. We've been planning this a long time . . . What?! You're going out with Elaine! Elaine who? . . . When did you turn loverboy? . . . Can't you go out with her next weekend? . . . I don't care if she's *soooo* cute . . . We've been planning this a long time . . . "

That weekend, instead of fishing up in the mountains with Rich, you're cutting grass for your dad. Fun, right?

What happened the last time you felt let down?

_____

_____

When Your Friends Laugh It Up at Your Expense

You beg your mom not to send you to school. You fake sick. You play dead. You threaten murder, suicide, terrorism. Nothing works. You arrive at school just before the bell rings.

You walk into class trying to turn invisible. (You're a little on the anorexic side, but invisible you ain't.) As you come down the aisle you notice your girlfriends' eyes bug out. Then you hear the worst sound you could ever hear in your entire life at this point — laughter.

Where'd you get your hair done? Acme Electric Company? HA HA HA HA HA HA! What color is that anyway? Fluorescent green? HA HA HA HA HA HA! What on earth built that nest on your head? HA HA HA HA!

You sit there, doing everything you know to hold back the tears. Fluorescent green may look good on Patti Punker, but not you. You wanted your hair to look like it had really bleached out in the sun during the summer, so you scraped together some money and risked letting the hairdresser bleach it a little — just a little, you told her.

She didn't just goof up your hair; she ruined your life.

What was the worst time you felt rejected?

Someone Understands

Jesus knows how it feels when people leave you out, let you down and laugh at you, because He has experienced all three. Take a close look at what Jesus went through in just twenty-four hours.

Let Down

Matthew 26:36-56 records Jesus' stay in the Garden of Gethsemane on the eve of His death. Grieved and distressed, He gathered His disciples to pray with Him. Jesus had spent three years with these men. They were His closest friends. He loved them deeply. Now, more than ever before, He needed them.

Read Matthew 26:36-56. List the times that Jesus' friends let Him down.

verses 36-41 _____

verses 42-43 _____

verses 44-46 _____

verses 47-50 _____

verse 56 _____

Have you ever been in a crisis situation before? A situation where prayer became your first choice, not merely your last chance? I have experienced a crisis like that.

When my first child was born prematurely, his lungs hadn't developed, making his condition critical. The attending doctors said his chances of living through the night were slim.

Hearing this, I rushed to the waiting room where twelve of my closest friends had gathered to see our newborn baby. As I explained the situation, my friends dropped to their knees, one by one, and began to pray for my little boy. As the night wore on, I would periodically return to the waiting room to update them on his condition. Each time I found them praying. Each time I was encouraged.

How do you think I would have felt if I had found my friends sleeping in my time of crisis?

_____

_____

How did Jesus feel when He found His best friends sleeping? (Reread the verses before answering.)

_____

_____

Not only did Jesus' friends fall asleep on Him in His hour of need, but one of them, Judas Iscariot, betrayed Him. Judas sold out the best friend a person could ever have for fifteen measly bucks. What an insult!

Perhaps it's happened to you. You tell your friend your deepest secret, like who you would like to date, and the next day at school it's all over campus.

Describe a time when you've been betrayed and how you felt:

_____

_____

Now multiply that 1,000,000 times to come close to how Jesus might have felt. But notice verse 50. In spite of Judas' betrayal, what did Jesus call Judas?

_____

What do you think was the tone of Jesus' voice when He called him this?

      ☐ sarcasm   ☐ hate

      ☐ disbelief   ☐ anger

      ☐ love   ☐ apathetic

As the guards arrested Jesus, the disciples hightailed it as quickly as they could. They probably thought, *I'm not hanging around to find out what happens. I might be next.* Whatever they were thinking, it's obvious they were more concerned for themselves than for Jesus.

How much do you think this hurt Jesus?

_____

_____

Laughed At

Later that morning Jesus found Himself on the Porch of Pilate. The Jews needed Pilate's permission to kill Jesus. You will find the story in Matthew 27:22-31. Read it and answer these questions.

What was Jesus guilty of?

_____

How did they punish Jesus?

verse 26 _____

verse 28 _____

verse 29 _____

verse 30 _____.

Have you ever really though about what Jesus went through?

The Roman soldier administering the scourge would have a whip of three or more thongs. The thongs would not be very long in length, but on the end of each of these thongs would be a sharp implement of stone metal or jagged bone. The person doing the scourging would hit the victim about the base of his neck and quickly pull the thongs, with the sharp implements imbedded in the flesh, down the length of his back. One medical authority stated that between the eighteenth and twenty-fifth lash the victim would have his skin torn completely off his back.[1]

Imagine Jesus, His back ripped open by the scourging, inch long thorns driven into His scalp and face, covered with blood and the soldiers' spit.

How would you feel seeing someone like this?

_____

_____

The soldiers, instead of feeling sorry for Jesus, mocked Him. What does it mean to mock someone? (Check it out in a dictionary if you need to.)

_____

_____

Left Out

Jesus, weak from the beating and a lack of sleep and food, was forced to carry His own cross to Golgotha. There, the soldiers drove stakes into His wrists and feet, then raised Him up on the cross.

In less than twenty-four hours, Jesus had been let down by His twelve closest friends, laughed at by His enemies and nailed to a cross for a crime He didn't commit. But the worst rejection was still to come.

Read Matthew 27:32-50. Who rejects Jesus in verse 46?

_____

The Creator of this universe, the Father God, the source of all love and goodness, had to reject His Son, Jesus Christ. No worse rejection exists.

What could make God reject His own Son? Sin. Romans 5:8 puts it this way: "God demonstrated His own love toward us, in that while we were yet sinners, Christ died for us." When Jesus accepted the guilt of everyone's sin, God the Father, though He had been with and loved Jesus for all eternity, had to reject Him. God allows no unholy person in His presence, not even His Son.

How did this make Jesus feel? (Reread verse 46.)

_____

_____

Jesus was rejected by

- His friends in the Garden of Gethsemane
- His foes at the Porch of Pilate
- His father on the Cross of Calvary

Do you think anyone has ever been more rejected, hurt or lonely?

Jesus knows what it's like when people leave you out, let you down, laugh it up at your expense. He understands how you feel when you are rejected, hurt and lonely.

Because it's likely that sometime someone will reject you, you need to know how to deal with that situation. Learn to respond to rejection the way Jesus did.

The Right Rejection Reaction

Jesus is Lord. He is Lord today and He was Lord two thousand years ago when He was rejected. Because He is Lord, He could have responded to His rejection any way He wanted. Yet when one of His disciples took out his sword and started whittling on the ear of the high priest's slave, Jesus told the disciple that He didn't need a little pocketknife to protect Him. He could call down 72,000 angels (a legion) to beat the living daylights out of those guys if he wanted. (I wish He had. Or at least He could have zapped them once or twice with a small-size lightning bolt.)

But He didn't.

Let's go back to the scene at the cross. Everyone made fun of Him—the chief priests, the scribes, the elders, the spectators, even the two robbers who were there just hanging around. Matthew 26 says everyone passed by hurling abuse and mocking Him.

Now if I could do anything, like Jesus could, I would have immediately, if not sooner, turned the first guy who laughed at me into a donkey. Not his whole body, just his head. Then we would see who they laughed at.

But Jesus didn't.

Not only that, but Jesus refused to give in to feeling sorry for Himself. Jesus never held a pity party.

Jesus was different. He refused to be motivated by revenge, hate, bitterness, anger or self-pity. You can be different, too. Through the power of the Holy Spirit living inside of you, you can respond like Jesus.

What was Jesus' right rejection reaction? He

- refused to get bitter,
- reached out in love, and
- raced to the best friend of all.

Let's check them out.

Refuse to Get Bitter

The last thing you want to do to those friends who reject you is to forgive them. Forget them—yes! Forgive them—NO! Yet that is exactly what Jesus did.

As the nails went through His hands, the physical pain was excruciating, but the fact that the people He loved were rejecting Him hurt just as badly, if not worse.

Read Luke 23:33-34. What was Jesus' response to those who crucified Him?

_____

_____

What does it mean to forgive someone?

_____

_____

What keeps you from forgiving the people who hurt you?

_____

_____

Forgiveness is tough, but living with hurt, bitterness and anger is worse. No one likes to be around a bitter person. You may think you're getting even by holding a grudge, but you're not. It only keeps you from enjoying your friends (the ones you're mad at *and* the ones you're not mad at). The first step to making the best of friendships involving rejection is to forgive your friends.

Digging Deeper

In John 21:1-17 Jesus communicates His continued friendship with Peter despite Peter's betrayal earlier. How would Peter and Jesus have felt if they never reconciled?

_____

_____

To forgive those who hurt you, pray this prayer from your heart:

Lord Jesus, You, and only You, could possibly understand

how I feel. It hurts bad, Lord, real bad. But I don't want to stay bitter, hurt and angry. Nor do I want to continue feeling sorry for myself. I want to respond like You did. By the power of the Holy Spirit within me, I forgive _____ for anything and everything he has ever done to me. By your heavenly power I choose to love him as You loved those who rejected You.

In Your Name Lord Jesus, Amen.

Reach Out in Love

When someone rejects you, and you respond out of your hurt, you will generally follow one of two routes. Either you put up a wall to avoid further hurt (and refuse to reach out to anyone), or you do *anything* to make friends because you hate the loneliness.

Hurt ← **Rejection** → **Hurt**

Fear of Hurt	Fear of Loneliness
Wall of Protection	Clinging to Others

The problem is, neither response will make you feel better or restore the friendship.

One day, in front of the whole class, one of my best friends made fun of my jeans being too short. I was mortified. I held a grudge for a long time. But even longer than that I refused to get close to him again.

Nobody likes being hurt. If you keep from getting close to people, you avoid being hurt. Some people carry this to an extreme. They get rejected by one close friend, then another, then another. Each time the pain intensifies, and finally they say, "Never again," refusing to reach out to anyone. They become a recluse.

On the other hand, people who do *anything* to make friends usually end up only making fools of themselves. They strive to be a people-pleaser, no matter what the cost. Eventually, they'll find that while they know a lot of people, they have few true friends.

Jesus wasn't motivated by hurt or anger or loneliness in His response to rejection. Read Luke 23:39-43. Jesus, nearly at the end of His life, after suffering nothing but rejection and pain for the last twenty-four hours, refused to think of Himself, and instead reached out to the thief hanging on the cross beside Him. Jesus was motivated by love. Even while dying He reached out not to *have* friends, but to *be* a friend.

Only with the power of the Holy Spirit will you be able to reach out in love to those who reject you. To be filled with the Spirit's power, pray a prayer like this:

> Lord Jesus, I want to love people the way You love people. I want to do this even if I'm rejected like You were rejected. Lord, I'm too weak to love like this by myself. Fill me with Your Holy Spirit, so I can love with Your love. Lord Jesus, love my friends through me.
>
> In Your name I pray, Amen.

Race to the Best Friend of All

Perhaps the worst part about being rejected is the loneliness you feel. Even if you have forgiven your friend and reached out in love, your loneliness doesn't just automatically disappear. It takes time. How do you get through it?

Life offers only one cure for loneliness: friendship. And there's one friendship that's even better than a Jonathan-and-David type friendship. It's a friendship that will never leave you feeling lonely.

Where can you find a friend like that? In the Lord Jesus Christ. He's the best friend of all.

Read Luke 23:44-46. Where did Jesus turn in His loneliness?

_____

_____

Are you lonely? You don't have to be. Jesus Christ, and only Jesus Christ, can meet all of your needs for love and acceptance. If you have never experienced His love, acceptance, forgiveness and friendship, you can right now. Simply pray this prayer:

Lord Jesus, I'm lonely. I'm in need of love. Please forgive me for my sins, come into my heart and be the best friend I've always wanted. Thank You Lord for dying on the cross to make this possible. Thank You for promising to never leave me or forsake me.

I love You Lord, Amen.

If you prayed this prayer, sign your name and put today's date below:

Name _____

Date _____

The next time you are lonely, race to Jesus Christ. Spend time with Him. Allow Him to meet your needs. Discover for yourself that you never have to be lonely again.

Jesus Christ, the very best friend of all.

Making the Best of Them

1. How do you respond when your friends:

Let you down?_____

Leave you out? _____

Laugh it up at your expense? _____

2. What new insight have you learned about the rejection of Jesus?

_____

_____

_____

3. If anyone has rejected you recently, how will you do the following?

Refuse to stay bitter: _____

_____

Reach out in love: _____

_____

Race to the best friend of all: _____

_____

Memorize Proverbs 18:24

_____
1. Source unknown.